Your life is a gift

Lewis Parkes

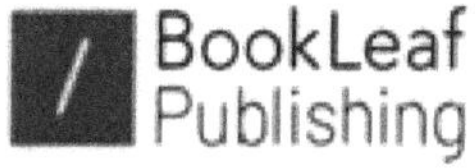

Presentation by *BookLeaf Publishing*

Web: www.bookleafpub.com

E-mail: info@bookleafpub.com

ISBN: 9789357211093

First edition 2022

DEDICATION

Dedicated to my partner and children with
much love and good feelings. Thank you for all
the support and love you give to me and each
other always.

PREFACE

This is the first time I've shared my creations with whoever chooses to see them. I hope they're enjoyed. A few might resonate with some readers and if they do I hope you are well. The front cover art is also painted and designed by me.

What is love

I could ask you my darling
What is love
You could hold my hand
And point above
It's the stars and beyond
You might say
It's the looking back
On a special day
It has no boundaries
It has no end
It's yours to give
'Til the very end
But what is love
Where does it start
You look at me
And touch my heart
It's deep inside
I hear you say
It's always been
Since that very day
The day you saw
My loving smile
That's where loves been
All the while
So what's 'In love'

It's everything
That we are in now
And have always been

Angel

Fifty years of life behind me
Fifty I hope ahead
Many things were there to test me
For some my tears were shed
I was told of angels
They watch over you
To help you find the way
I prayed to the stars
As I looked to the sky
That I'd meet my Angel one day

I read it in books
And the questions I asked
Went unanswered on how we'd meet
How would I find her
What are the chances
I swore never to admit defeat
So I went with the flow
But not letting go
I would wait, relax and just see
Now my Angel was there
Though I never knew where
She'd reveal when I'm ready to see

'Twas a time when I never expected

'Twas a time when again I could love
When she came to my life on an invite
Light shone down on her right from above
I knew not at the time of this Angel
But I felt how my feelings were strong
I knew nothing but still felt the beauty
My instincts I trust were not wrong
So I smiled and put my arms around her
I felt honesty, goodness, no pain
When we parted I wanted her close to me
To feel this all over again

My Angel is now always with me
My life she was sent to save
My Angel I fell in love with
And her love I will take to my grave
But a life I look forward to living
The life will be rich and long
I decided to give her my heart and soul
From day one my choice wasn't wrong
I look at my Angel and smile now
I look at my Angel and love
My Angel is beautiful and true to me
She's my heartbeat that plays like a song

Your lives are a gift

I want to say thank you
Your lives are a gift
Surrounded in warmth
My spirit does lift
For the times that we have
Are all very nice
'Cause I love you each day
I'll love you for life
No borders no boundaries
Will keep us apart
I love you my sons
With all of my heart
Yesterday, today
Even tomorrow
I picture your faces
And a smile always follows
We might not be certain
Of the world that we're in
But we know where it started
Where ours did begin
And where it is heading
I'm sure we all know
The love I will nurture
The bond it will grow
It's ending is never

That much we can see
For it's us now forever
Always my sons and me

I am not my best

I may not feel my best right now
I may be in some pain
I may be quiet or sometimes grumpy
But I love you all the same
I'm lucky to have you care for me
I'm lucky that you are there
Because still I'm happy as can be
With you my life I'll share
My life's now full of richness
But it doesn't cost a thing
The rains of hardness run away
As I shelter under wing
I long to pay you back one day
Hence the life I plan is long
To look after and care for you my loves
Whenever somethings wrong
For now I'll thank you for all you do
For laughter after tears
For the comfort, shelter and all else
And protection from my fears
You saved me on the day we met
My life now filled with light
That moment your hand slipped into mine
For us the future's bright

The Boat

The boat was never
meant to be
No lonely life
on tideless sea
The escape, the hope
Expecting fun
A cool sea breeze
An Ocean sun
Memories, the memories
They end once day is done

Calm creeps in
Brings with it fear
Lonely horizons
Another year
Under sun and under moon
Hear them play the same old tune
Vision fades
It takes its toll
Across the seas of frozen fortitude
He'd hoped to find his soul

The house

I wake in my house
All alone
But this place has changed
This place has grown
Once just a house
A place to live
Then a homely touch
You came to give
You opened the windows
And then the doors
You brought it light
I then I saw
No longer a house
It's now a home
Your touch remains
And I'm not alone
I look around
It's you I see
In everything
That is around me
A home with love
There is no doubt
But the love is more
When you're about

Cause to smile

Are you still in bed
Will you lay there a while
Are you thinking of us
Does it cause you to smile
Are you cocooned in your duvet
All warm and snug
Do you wish I were there
Are you craving a hug
Can you stay there all day
Just dreaming your dreams
Where true love is real
And is what it seems
'Til I make my way over
To be there with you
We can lay there together
And make dreams come true
Are you still in bed
Will you wait there for me
It's the one place right now
That I want to be
There in your arms
All close and tight
It's where I belong
And I'll be there tonight
So stay there in bed

And dream for a while
I will picture your face
And your beautiful smile
It will help get me through
The long day ahead
'Til I'm there next to you
In your snug little bed

The things I miss when I'm not with you

Looking into your eyes at a love that's true
Having our cuddles as the perfect two
Seeing your smile and mischievous look
Snuggled up tight while reading a book
Learning new things about who we are
Making new plans to travel afar
Laughter, jumps and sometimes tears
The calming chats to calm my fears
The long loving looks, the random kisses
These are the things that I, my heart and soul
misses

Thinking of you

So I'm thinking of you
I'm thinking of us
You are the one I can truly trust
With my heart
With my love
With my mind, body, soul
You entered my life
And you made me whole

You're the wind in my hair
The earth at my feet
You're the laughter, the tears
My very heartbeat
When I breathe
It is you
Who gives me my breath
It is you
Who will bring me life after death

For our love is forever
It always will be
Our eyes were wide open
For each other to see
On the night that we met

You gave me new life
My girlfriend, now fiancée
And one day my wife

I miss you

I miss you
I might say to you
I miss you
You should hear
I miss you, is meant to make you smile
Not to cause you any fear
For to miss is not a negative thing
To miss says somethings there
To miss the closeness, love and fun
It's not just not being there
It's the smile, the touch the glancing look
Playing piano, reading a book,
Seeing that smile, hearing your voice
Missing you is never a choice
Sharing our warmth, feeling your hand
I'm happy to walk, I'm happy to stand
Side by side or face to face
We fitted neatly in that space
I miss you
I will say to you
Because I love you so
But missing you just shows to me
Our love will always grow

A short message

A short message for when you rise
I dream of the light on your beautiful eyes
I feel the warmth when your hand touches mine
And if I could that's when I'd pause time
I'd hold you close
I hold you tight
I'd stay there with you
Where everything's right

30 miles

Thirty miles to the woman I love
That's what I think when I get in my car
Thirty miles to the woman I love
The journey isn't really that far

The engine starts with a pop and a fart
And off I drive with a smile
I think of not distance just the woman I love
As I drive there mile by mile

I see the tunnel, the bridge
The traffic is light
I'll see it again soon
I can't stay for the night
For restrictions have said
Don't travel afar
Thirty miles? I say
In my little car?
Well that's not too far
I think in my head
To spend some time
With the woman I'll wed

Fifteen miles now to the woman I'll wed
The tunnel is now long behind

Fifteen miles now to the woman I'll wed
All the time she is there in my mind

I'm getting there darling
It won't be too long
Turn on the radio
They're playing our songs
The ones that have meaning
'Woman' I hear
Some can bring smiles
And some bring forth tears
I think of the piano
The place where you play
A warmth inside me
On the sofa I lay
All sorts in my mind
On my journey to you
From cuddles and kisses
To even a brew

No more miles now to the woman I love
Just one corner and I'm at your drive
No more miles now to the woman I love
My heart quickens as I arrive

Our time together
Will always go fast
No matter to that
Our love is steadfast

For we make the most
Of the time that we get
Chilling indoors
Or out in the wet
I'll always love you
And make that 'short' drive
To the woman I'll wed
Who keeps me alive
With a passion for things
That are simple and free
The short journey brings happiness
To you and to me

The rain

So here I sit
In my chair
I am here
And you are there
Still under the same sky
We feel the rain
As it runs down our cheeks
It's natural, no shame
Don't be afraid
When the rain is flowing
It's there to show feelings
Of a love that is growing

What do we know
About the rain
For some there is joy
For some sorrow or pain
We know not all rain
Falls from above
But showers and engulfs us
Quite similar to love

What do we know
About love that is deep
Like the sound of the rain

It prevents us from sleep
We know not beginnings
Or where it will end
True love is like raindrops
You can't break it or bend

So the love can flow
In many ways
But rain comes and goes
Sometimes just for the day
Love should be constant
Trickling slowly then fast
Engulfing you wholly
With passion that lasts
Unwavering feelings of love
All for you
As I sit here, thinking
Wishing one was now two

The rain has now stopped
Again will it start?
A lone drop on my cheek
Not from sky but from heart
To me it is rain
To some it's a tear
For it's not from pain
Or anguish or fear
It's the tiniest bundle
Rolling down from above

Containing all feelings
But most of all love

Feelings of yesterday

The feelings of yesterday
Still fresh in my mind
The passion
The love
Our bodies entwined
My hands on your hips
Move down to your thighs
Looking up at your face
Deeply into your eyes
To feel you on top
To see your chest heave
As euphoria escapes
The heavier you breathe
The sounds that you make
It's near to an end
Our bodies contorted
The message it sends
It says we are one
So we lay there so close
Share heartbeats and breathing
We've now had our dose
Of love, of passion
Of feelings of two
One who loves me
And one who loves you

So the feelings of yesterday
Will be on my mind
Today and tomorrow
Until our next time

My beautiful

My beautiful, beautiful
Wife to be
You encourage, enable
Allow me to see
The good things ahead
A life that's great
My love, my lover
My true soulmate
One day I know
This pain will pass
Unlike our love
That will always last
You change my aches
To smiles and laughter
You're my joy, my warmth
My happy ever after

The briefest moment

Was the briefest of moments
That's all it took
My heart skipped a beat
My world suddenly shook
Was the look in your eyes
The touch of your skin
In a car park in Bexley
I felt it begin
My heart was racing
After our first kiss
An opportune moment
I dared not to miss
A gamble for me
Before saying goodbye
A message of wanting
As I looked in your eyes

The river

There are times when our feelings
Don't go with the flow
Not loving any less
Just sometimes don't show
A lake filled with love
Is a lake standing still
'Til the river it finds
Where the love will then fill
For miles it will stretch
Breaching currents and tides
Searching for the one
Unsure where she hides
Sometimes deep sometimes shallow
Can be short, can be long
She hides at the mouth
Where the river is strong
With arms open wide
This river she trusts
She accepts every drop
As the bed dries to dust
But the river continues
To flow in her heart
It carries her back
To true love at the start

Sometimes I'd think

I would often stand by the kitchen sink
Pointless staring
But sometimes I'd think
Today I thought
Now what is love
A feeling inside, outside, up above?
There are no rules to how we feel
No questions, conditions
When the feeling's real
Love surrounds us in all different ways
It get us up and through the day
To know there's someone
So special, so grand
Where love's in the fingers
When holding hands
A look in the eyes
Tells a thousand truths
Of how we feel
How love can soothe
Just a few things I thought
By the kitchen sink
Love is us
That's what I think

Under the same sky

I look up at the sky
You look down from the plane
I smile at the thought
When I'll see you again

As the distance grows
And we're miles apart
We'll still feel the beating
Of each other's warm hearts

Under one setting sun
Under one rising moon
I'll settle to sleep
Knowing I'll see you soon

For the time apart's temporary
And although we'll feel sad
When you're back in my arms
We both will be glad

I look up at the sky
As your plane comes to land
Hoping soon you'll be with me
As we walk hand in hand

I look up at the sky
This time no plane to see
I look up at the sky
As you stand here with me

Now you're in my arms
We both look above
We know distance is nothing
When you're truly in love

Things about you

Those soft lips, the passionate kiss
The look in those beautiful eyes
They change colour from time to time
The love they can't disguise

The touch of your hand
A long seaside walk
The sound of your voice
Whenever we talk

You shouting boo
And making me jump
Turns to laughter
Never the hump

The knowing your thoughts
And you knowing mine
Making the coffee
Or pouring the wine

The eggs are a given
With pepper and salt
The routine we have
Without second thought

Across the table
Your beautiful face
The love that we have
Filling the place

Sometimes tears, sometimes jokes
It's all open and free
With you being you and
Me being me

I leave knowing that
There is part of me there
I take part of you with me
Your true love and care

The smell of your perfume
On tissue to say
I'll be back in your arms
Before it fades away

I'm always there darling
And you're always here
In my thoughts, heart and soul
Where I hold you most dear

Birth haiku

Birth brings the sunshine
Daily smiles and happiness
Sound and peaceful sleep

www.ingramcontent.com/pod-product-compliance
Lightning Source LLC
LaVergne TN
LVHW010946200726

843509LV00013B/2296